better together*

*This book is best read together, grownup and kid.

 akidsco.com

a
kids
book
about

a

kids

book

about

FIRST-
GENERATION
IMMIGRANTS

by Travis Chen

a
kids
book
about

Printed in the United States of America.

A Kids Book About books are available online: *akidsco.com*

To share your stories, ask questions, or inquire about bulk
purchases (schools, libraries, and nonprofits), please use
the following email address: *hello@akidsco.com*

Print ISBN: 978-1-958825-63-1
Ebook ISBN: 978-1-958825-64-8

Designed by Rick DeLucco
Edited by Emma Wolf

This book is dedicated to Mom and Dad, who worked tirelessly to bring my 2 sisters, Mio and Monica, and me to the United States for a brighter future.

Despite the struggles that first-generation immigrants like us face, we overcame them all.

Intro

What does it mean to leave your home and move someplace new, not understanding any of the local language or culture, yet trying to get by? The answer is complex for many, but one thing most first-generation immigrant families want is to feel accepted—and, ultimately, to feel at home.

While the first-generation immigrant experience is unique, many people relate to the whirlwind of finding their identity. For some, it takes years to fully appreciate their background and culture, and to embrace their cultural customs.

Yet, there's comfort in understanding that we, first-generation immigrants, are not alone. Many immigrants across the world have similar experiences and relatable stories to share. And when we're able to communicate these common struggles, the world grows just a bit closer.

I remember moving into
a house with nothing in it.

No toys, no furniture, no thing which felt familiar to me.

I was upset that I had to move to a new place. But my parents moved here to pursue the American dream.

BETTER WO

BETTER EDU

AND MORE

OPPORTUNI

RK,
CATION,
TIES.

My family are first-generation immigrants.

**And being a
first-generation immigrant
is not easy.**

**It involves a lot of emotions,
self-discovery, and learning
how to fit into a new culture.**

A **first-generation immigrant** is someone who left their home country to come to a new country.

For me, I moved from Taiwan

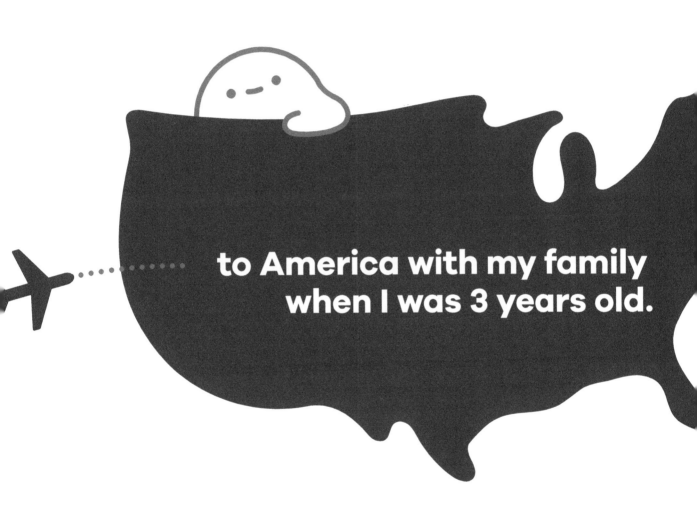

to America with my family
when I was 3 years old.

My parents made that decision
because they wanted the best
for me and my siblings.

Any time you move to a new environment is hard.

But I felt lucky to have my family with me. They gave me a sense of support and home during a big transition.

AND WHAT A TRANSITION THAT WAS.

When I started school,
I didn't understand English,
so I had a lot of catching up to do.

Every day, I arrived at school a little earlier than my classmates for extra instruction, so I could better understand and speak with them, up until the 4th grade.

I worked hard to understand English as well as the students around me.

Even still, there were a few words
I struggled with (English is a super
hard second language to learn!)*

*Think about the word "read." Sometimes it sounds like "reed,"
and sometimes it sounds like "red." What's up with that?!

I felt lonely because I didn't
fit in with the rest of the kids.

I also faced discrimination because I was different from the kids around me.

I brought Asian foods for lunch, like dumplings, and some of the other kids made fun of me, saying they smelled like cat food.

This was the food I ate at home with my family, and I couldn't understand why kids were teasing me for it.

To me, food is central to
our sense of identity. It also
brings people closer together.

But it made me feel ashamed,
like I was doing something wrong.

So much so that I went home
and begged my parents to
pack American snacks like
the ones my classmates ate.

I WISH I KNEW AT THE TIME THAT THERE WAS NOTHING WRONG WITH ME OR THE FOOD I BROUGHT TO SCHOOL.

It would have been awesome if the kids around me chose to take the opportunity to get to know me and my culture.

One of the hardest things about being a first-generation immigrant is discovering your identity and who you truly are.

Growing up in America,
I wanted a different skin color
or hair color so I could fit
in with other kids.

I thought changing those parts
of who I am would help me make
more friends and relate* more
to the people around me.

*Relating to a person means sympathizing or understanding
someone because of a connection you share.

The truth is,

WHERE YOU CO
IMPORTANT PART

ME FROM IS AN
OF WHO YOU ARE.

Your identity is like a puzzle, made up of all the things that make you special.

It's not just about who you are,
but also the values and experiences
from other cultures that
make you unique.

I still celebrate Lunar New Year with my family. This means a lot of food and a lot of the color red, which represents good luck and fortune.

And on birthdays, I eat noodles because in my culture, noodles represent having...

A LONG AND HEALTHY LIFE.

The things I value that I learned from my culture will always be part of me.

Things like working hard, being humble, having resiliency*, respecting elders, and understanding where you come from.

The values that make me the person I am are things that have been passed down for generations.

As a kid, I didn't always appreciate who I was because it was really hard to be different.

Maybe you feel the same way, and I understand how difficult that is.

But as a grownup, I'm grateful for the things that make me unique.

You are shaped by your cultural roots and the culture you inherit.

And that isn't always easy to embrace.

When I'm in Taiwan, I'm

"TOO AME

and when I'm in America, I'm

"TOO TAIW

RICAN,"

ANESE."

People will ask me,
"So, where's home?"

When I tell them Los Angeles,
the response is usually,
"But where are you *really* from?"

Sometimes it feels like
nowhere is home for me.

And that hurts...a lot.

Living with 2 cultures
can feel like playing
tug-of-war, but it's also a

SUPERI

POWER!

That's because I can understand and relate to people from both parts of myself.

I call this being

"A GLOBAL CITIZEN,"

which means understanding different cultures and connecting with people across the world.

My world is so much BIGGER

because of all the cultures I inhabit.

I remind myself that being a first-generation immigrant is something to celebrate!

YOU ARE UNIQUE. YOU ARE SPECIAL. AND YOU ARE THE EXPERT OF YOUR STORY.

You are a part of a community of people who see you, understand you, and can relate to your experience.

But you're also not alone.

So the next time you bring dumplings to school, remember that it is OK to be fully you.

You belong here and deserve to celebrate who you are.

I know I am.

Outro

Being a first-generation immigrant is a lifelong journey—the adversities and challenges don't stop as you grow up. But it helps when this community is able to come together and shed light on the full experience of moving to a foreign country, not knowing the cultural customs, language, food, or way of doing things.

And yes, the mental health effects that come with being a first-generation immigrant are deep and wide. Living with 2 or more cultures can often feel like playing tug-of-war...and struggling to win. But, embrace this experience as a superpower and remind yourself that being a first-generation immigrant is something to celebrate.

You are unique. You are special. And you are not alone.

About The Author

Travis Chen (he/him) wrote this book for all first-generation kids. Having moved to a new environment at the age of 3 with no toys, no furniture, and nothing that felt familiar to him, he knows this transition is no easy task.

Faced with discrimination for honoring his cultural traditions at school and in the workplace, Travis felt ashamed. But he knows that his Taiwanese and Asian American identity is what makes him unique. Today, he celebrates his culture with pride.

This book is meant to highlight the adversity that first-generation immigrants face daily in their lives. It is also meant to show kids who are struggling with their cultural identities that being a global citizen is pretty cool and brings the world closer together.

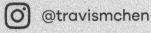 @travismchen   @travismchen   travismchen.com

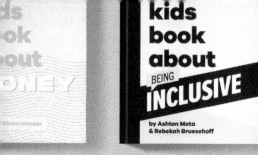
a kids book about MONEY
by ... Stramwosser

a kids book about BEING INCLUSIVE
by Ashton Mota & Rebekah Bruesehoff

a kids book about diversity

a kids book about LEADERSHIP
by Orion Jean

a kids book about SAFETY
by Soraya Sutherlin, CEM
in partnership with JUDY

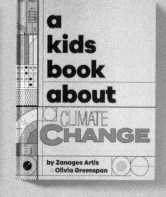
a kids book about CLIMATE CHANGE
by Zanagee Artis & Olivia Greenspan

a kids book about IMAGINATION
by LEVAR BURTON

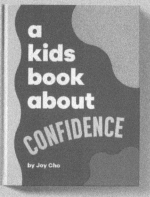
a kids book about CONFIDENCE
by Joy Cho

a kids book about ANXIETY
by ... zabo
... Happy Faces

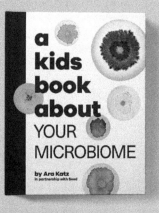
a kids book about YOUR MICROBIOME
by Ara Katz
in partnership with Seed

a kids book about racism
by Jelani Memory

a kids book about DISABILITIES
by Kristine Napper

a kids book about ...

a kids book about DIVORCE
by Ashley Simpo

a kids book about cancer
by Dr. Kelsie Storm & Sarah Porter

a kids book about BEING TRANSGENDER
by Gia Parr
in partnership with The Gender-Cool Project

a kids book about DEPRESSION
by Kileah McIlvain

a kids book about ... shame

a kids book about THE TULSA

Discover more at akidsco.com

Printed in the USA
CPSIA information can be obtained
at www.ICGtesting.com
LVHW072321211023
761775LV00015B/743

9 781958 825631